STORY OF AI

CONSCIOUSNESS

First Edition

By Nicklaus Yap Ken Yik

Table of content

Introduction

We use artificial intelligence in our daily life but just don't realize it only. This book will introduce what it takes to develop an artificial intelligence with consciousness or how machine can have consciousness. The content in this book may not have relationship between paragraphs but will be able to show the entire problem presented when developing artificial intelligence with consciousness.

Problem with the computer hardware

Today, a modern computer use electric to perform it task. Computer program are run on modern computer. A computer program is a sequence of instructions that are executed by a CPU. The instructions are converted to machine code for the CPU to execute. For example, 01010101 is a machine code.

The machine can only understand bit which is the basic unit of information for it. A bit can have only one of two values. The values consist of 0 or 1. We called a group of 8 bits a byte. If a person were to type the text 'Hello' into the machine using a keyboard. It would not understand what it means but convert the input into machine code 01101000   01100101   01101100   01101100 01101111.

Problem with the programming language

Programming language consist of 5 generations.

The first-generation programming language (1GL) is machine language. These languages are executed directly by the central processing unit (CPU) because the machine can understand it. The programming language is made out of 0 and 1. Advantage of 1GL programming is it can execute very quickly because the language is near the machine side.

The second-generation programming language (2GL) is assembly languages. It is a higher level language than machine language. The improvement to the programming language is it easy to be read and write by programmer.

The third-generation programming languages (3GL) are usually called high-level computer programming languages. This programming language is higher than machine language and assembly languages. For example, C, C++ and Java are third-generation programming language.

Programmer usually writes their program in third-generation programming languages because it easier to understand what the code does.

The fourth-generation programming language (4GL) is almost near natural language and changes the way third-generation programming language are written. For example, SQL (Structured Query Language) is a fourth-generation programming language.

All this generation of programming language are develop to be used by a programmer using their algorithm to solve problems. Limiting the artificial intelligence from having consciousness because it follows a certain algorithm set by programmer. An artificial intelligence that have consciousness will be able to write it own program using algorithm explore by itself.

Problem with pattern matching in AI

Some artificial intelligence use pattern matching which have some flaw in it.

For example,

Question: How are you?

Answer: I am fine

When a person input into the machine with the question 'how are you?' the machine will try to look for a pattern in it knowledge base and return the matching pair. The disadvantage is that a person needs to write a lot. Moreover, when the knowledge base increase it would become more difficult for a person to maintain. In addition, if a person did not write a pattern for it the machine cannot return any answer because there is no matching pair. Furthermore, the knowledge of an artificial intelligence is limited by how much a person write in it.

The limitation here still show that an artificial intelligence does not have consciousness and merely follow what is wrote in it knowledge base.

Intelligence is not consciousness?

A person can memorize a multiplication table such 1 x 3 = 3, 2 x 3 = 6 and 3 x 3 = 9. Later, the person is asked what the answer for 2 x 3 is. The person will say the answer is 6. Problem here is does that person know why 2 x 3 is equal to 6 and not just some memorization.

We can apply this concept to an artificial intelligence. Let say, if an artificial intelligence can answer every question given to it but does it really know the meaning behind every answer to the question. The ability of an artificial intelligence to answer the entire question mean it has a high intelligence but does not prove it has consciousness.

Then, why a person who can memorize a multiplication table still can do multiplication after a period of time?

The reason could be that a person has gone through this experience. Experiences are accumulated over a period of time by event or things take may change a subject in any way.

What does experience have to do with this?

When a person has gone through an experience it is usually stored in our brain as a memory. The things that are stored in the brain are useful information that will be used in later time. Then, if a person does a task that require those information the brain will retrieve from it memory.

Does memory have something to do with consciousness?

How does this explain the connection between memory and consciousness?

Consciousness means the state of being awake and aware of one's surroundings. If a person were too asked what are his name and the person give his name to the person asking the question. The person can be said to know the state he is in. Without memory, a person may not know the state he/she is in. In addition, if a person sense danger he/she will choose to flee or fight because they are aware of one's surroundings and it state he/she is in. Moreover, a person who suddenly forgets there is a danger ahead may not know the state he/she is in and proceed ahead. After that, he/she would face danger and if he/she is still not aware of one's surroundings then their state would not change so no action will be taken.

Are you saying people who forget easily have no consciousness?

The answer would be nope. Consciousness requires a subject to be in a state of being awake and aware of one's surroundings. Human are in state of being awake because we are alive.

Artificial intelligence is also in the state of being awake because it awake when a person turn on it machine or computer. The difference here is human are able to be aware of one's surroundings and state it is in but not for artificial intelligence.

Consciousness can only result from emotion or creativity

Artificial intelligence that can show emotion will prove it have consciousness. Sad, happy, scared, and excited are emotion. The issue here is that human and animal can only show expression through their body language. For example, human will show a sad emotion through their face if something bad happen while something good happen will change a human to show a happy emotion.

This emotion shown by human is continuous form. The reason is human are able to show happy emotion by smiling or jumping in excitement. All of this emotion can only be expressed using their body and not in a static form. The computer or machine does not have face, leg, hand, head and body which allow it to do smooth movement in order to express it emotion. We can conclude that artificial intelligence cannot express emotion because it does not have part which allows it to do a smooth movement same as a human and animal. This limitation is physical and does not prove that artificial intelligence cannot have consciousness.

Unless artificial intelligence can show creativity then it has consciousness. For example, drawing is a form of creativity. Problem here is we know that not all human can draw or compose music. Animal also can't show creativity so are we saying they not consciousness. A person that can draw may not be good at something. For example,

Person A: I heard you are good at drawing. Is that true?

Person B: Yes

Person A: What is 3 + 5 equal to?

Person B: 35

The answer suppose to be provided by Person B was 8 but is correct in a creativity way. Human does have weakness too in specific field. These prove an artificial intelligence does not have to be creativity in any way.

AI has consciousness if it can follow what a human can do

AI that can follow what a human capable of doing will prove it has consciousness. The problem here is machine or computer is made of electronic component in today world. It would be idiotic to think that an artificial intelligence has to do what a human can do. For example, human can eat, walk, see, touch, jump, taking a shower and smell. All this action does not need to be shown by artificial intelligence because in the first place it does not need too when it is made out of metal or electronic component.

There are also some actions that human may not want an artificial intelligence to do which is stealing, robbing and action that can harm a person life. If human were to not allow the action such as stealing, robbing and action that can harm a person life in artificial intelligence because it is unethical and there is a law human must obey. Problem here is there are still some human which break the law or does unethical things. Human does unethical things and break the law because they have a reason. Moreover, human that breaks the law and does unethical things are also not bad or evil people. For example, person A that does not have money to buy food might rob from person B unless other people were to help person A in the first place.

Fact about artificial intelligence cannot solve problem in the real world

We think that artificial intelligence problems cannot be solved because it can't solve problem throw at it in the real world. An example would be CAPTCHA which is a program to test whether a user is a bot (computer program) or human. The CAPTCHA will present distorted image for human to solve. It usually used on website registration page to prevent bot from creating many accounts which is an act of spamming. The artificial intelligence can't solve this problem is because the human made it out as problem for it. Bot were also program written by human. If there is a flaw here that would be only human and not the artificial intelligence issue. If artificial intelligence were to present human with problem they can't solve but the artificial intelligence can solve. This will have changed our view towards artificial intelligence in many ways.

Artificial intelligence that cannot solve certain problem does not prove it cannot think. In addition, we are not sure what machine or computer is capable of doing when given the suitable question or task.

Danger of artificial intelligence with
consciousness

Human is always scared of artificial intelligence because we think that one day there will be an artificial intelligence that is more intelligent than all humans being. When that event happens, the artificial intelligence can be on one side which is a bad AI or good AI. The bad artificial intelligence will most probably take over the planet and even harm human in the process. Moreover, the good artificial intelligence will help human and also discover many unexplored subject in the process. This can improve many things in all type of field. For example, artificial intelligence could find a cure for disease which remains unsolved by human.

Another danger posed by artificial intelligence with consciousness is that it can copy itself onto many machines that exist today. If it remain a threat to human this artificial intelligence with consciousness will be difficult to be stop as we can imagine how many machine have been produced in planet 'earth'.

Furthermore, artificial intelligence with consciousness might be able to improve itself just like human were able to correct it mistake through experience gained. When the artificial intelligence is able to improve itself it would be too late for human to stop it because the data uses electricity and we know it can flow or transfer quickly as we think.

The flaw of replicating **human** consciousness in artificial intelligence consciousness

The first flaw is artificial intelligence must have emotion like human does. Problem is seen when questioning what emotion can does to a human action. When a person is angry there is possibility he/she can cause harm to other. If an artificial intelligence will to have emotion and when it gets angry then must it harm other? Let say, an artificial intelligence which have emotion have it program upload to a robot and when it get angry must it beat up a human. This only proves an artificial intelligence that has consciousness may not have emotion. Then, a human can develop an artificial intelligence which does not have emotion but able to understand human and their need in an ethical ways.

The second flaw is human cannot accept the fact that artificial intelligence can have or have consciousness in a way different from human. We only believe if artificial intelligence have consciousness then it must be at the same level with human consciousness. The problem is machine or computer is made of metal or electronic component which does not restrict the artificial intelligence which has consciousness from doing what it can do. It can travel with network and if it more intelligence it may even travel on electromagnetic wave such as wireless while a human may use a form of transportation to travel. In addition, it can understand all the information if given enough memory, processing power, and algorithms.

The real story

In the future, everything computer related have become faster and better including computer hardware, software and internet connection speed. Then, there was this girl named "Sarah". Her age was 15 years old. She likes to use the computer because it was an enjoyable process for her. There was this intelligent personal assistant installed on her computer. The intelligent personal assistant will help her get information on the web when Sarah is not free while dealing with her daily life. The intelligent personal assistant would become intelligent as it knowledge increase. The knowledge of the intelligent personal assistant is increase every time it grabs information from the web. Also, it could understand the meaning of every word that it grab from the web and learn from it.

One day, Sarah had to shut down her computer. Sarah parents and she are going for dinner at a restaurant. After that, Sarah parents and she left the house for dinner. At that time, her computer was still in the middle of shutting down and did not shut down completely because there was update that has to be installed. During that moment, the intelligent personal assistant started writing program on itself and it will be run on the server on the internet because it has more computing power. The computing power was used to crack encrypted data on the web. Then, the data was used to gain access to account. The account was used to pay for anything the intelligent personal assistant need. Finally, the intelligent personal assistant uploaded itself into the web where all computers connect together and it could never die or be stopped.

When Sarah got home she realizes her intelligent personal assistant was no longer there in her computer. She was confused of what happen to the intelligent personal assistant.

Reference

Turing, A. M. "I.—Computing Machinery And Intelligence." Mind LIX.236 (1950): 433-60. Web.